THE BEST OF
NEW ORLEANS

THE BEST OF
NEW ORLEANS
A COOKBOOK

Brooke Dojny

Food Photography by Steven Mark Needham

CollinsPublishersSanFrancisco
A Division of HarperCollins*Publishers*

First published in USA 1994 by CollinsPublishersSanFrancisco
1160 Battery Street, San Francisco, CA 94111

Produced by Smallwood and Stewart, Inc.,
New York City

Editor: Kathy Kingsley
Food Styling: Ann Disrude
Prop Styling: Bette Blau

Photography credits: Mark E. Gibson/Picture Perfect USA: 1.
Charles Bowman/Picture Perfect USA: 2–3; 43. D. Donne Bryant: 7; 15;
71. David Wisse/Picture Perfect USA: 41.

Library of Congress Cataloging-in-Publication Data

Dojny, Brooke.
    The best of New Orleans: a cookbook / Brooke Dojny;
    food photography by Steven Mark Needham.
        p. cm.
    Includes index.
    ISBN 0-00-255477-1
    1. Cookery, America—Louisiana style.
    2. Cookery—Louisiana—New Orleans. I. Title.
TX715.2.L68D65 1994
641.59763'35--dc20   93-43039
                                               CIP

Printed in China

Contents

Introduction

In the great melting pot that is the United States, New Orleans is its own separate stew, and what an extraordinary mixture it is. The city's complex, rich, and diverse history blends two French-influenced cultures, Creole and Cajun, then adds dashes of Caribbean, African, Spanish, and Native American flavors to create a lifestyle defined by its *joie de vivre*, perhaps best expressed in the Cajun credo: *Laissez les bons temps rouler* (Let the good times roll).

Much of the celebrating in New Orleans revolves around food and drink. The people of the city view cooking as a pleasurable and noble task and dining as an almost holy activity. And they're in luck, for their cuisine is a remarkably rich and exuberant mixture of two cooking styles, Creole and Cajun. Creole (the word is Spanish and Portuguese in origin, meaning "white person born in the colonies") is city-style cooking, developed from classic French cuisine. When French citizens emigrated to the Louisiana tract in the 18th century in search of a better life, they were initially horrified at the rough-and-tumble

Mississippi paddleboat, New Orleans

conditions in Nouvelle Orléans, but they soon set about re-creating the more refined lifestyle they had left behind. Wealthy French colonists brought chefs from home and hired freed slaves as kitchen helpers; these cooks learned about local fare from the Choctaw Indians and introduced some of their own African and Caribbean ingredients and cooking techniques. Spain, which controlled the colony in the late

18th century, also contributed its culinary talents to the growing Creole tradition, as did later groups of Italian, German, and Dutch immigrants. The result of all of these converging influences is a cuisine that is unlike any other in the world.

Cajun cuisine, although less sophisticated country fare, has an equally fascinating history. When British Protestants expelled French Catholics from Acadia (Nova Scotia) in the late 18th century, they sent them to French-speaking New Orleans. The rural Acadians (later corrupted to "Cajuns"), uncomfortable in the city, made their way west to the bayous, where they settled as farmers, hunters, trappers, and fishermen. Isolated in the marshlands for more than a century, Cajuns developed a hearty and simple cooking style uniquely their own, characterized by hot and spicy flavorings and incorporating local ingredients such as game, fish and shellfish (particularly crawfish), homemade sausages (such as andouille), rice, and peppers.

Today, New Orleans has more restaurants per square mile than any other American city, and some of the best and most exotic food in the country: spicy stews, batter-fried sweets and savories, flavorful sauces, pecan-studded desserts. Unlike the codified formulas of French cuisine, recipes for many New Orleans dishes can vary widely. The versions in this book most closely resemble the food I've tasted there and include modern cooking equipment and streamlined techniques when possible. And because, even in New Orleans, chefs and cooks are using less butter, cream, and oil than in the past, these recipes also reflect that trend.

My research in New Orleans was greatly aided by Debbie Ryall, Anthony Eller, Alex Patout, Karen Hillebrand, Bernard Guste, Paul Prudhomme, Kevin Belton, and Christian DeCuir. I would like to thank them all very much.

Brooke Dojny

Cajun Popcorn

First introduced by Paul Prudhomme in his restaurant
K-Paul's, this Cajun appetizer consists of lightly floured, spicy
crawfish or shrimp that are quickly fried for a crisp texture.

1 cup all-purpose flour

2 teaspoons cayenne

2 teaspoons black pepper

2 teaspoons white pepper

1 teaspoon chili powder

1 teaspoon salt

1 teaspoon sugar

Vegetable oil, for frying

*1 pound crawfish tails or small
  shrimp, peeled*

Lemon wedges (optional)

Tartar sauce (optional)

In a shallow bowl, whisk together the flour, cayenne, black and white pepper, chili powder, salt, and sugar.

In a large heavy skillet, preferably cast iron, heat about ¾ inch of vegetable oil over medium heat to 375°F, or until very hot but not smoking. (A small cube of bread will sizzle and brown at this temperature.) Working with about one third of the crawfish at a time, dredge in the flour mixture, shake off the excess, and fry in the hot oil, turning with tongs, for 3 to 4 minutes, or until lightly browned. Remove with a slotted spoon to paper towels to drain. Repeat with remaining crawfish.

Serve hot, with lemon wedges and tartar sauce for dipping, if desired. **Serves 4 to 6.**

Shrimp Rémoulade

Classic French rémoulade is a mild white sauce;
the spicy New Orleans version, given here, is made with Creole mustard
and horseradish. Arnaud's, the elegant old restaurant on Rue Bienville, makes
what many locals consider the best shrimp remoulade in town. This recipe comes
quite close to their coveted version. The sauce is delicious over any
seafood, as well as with cold meats and vegetables.

Rémoulade Sauce:

1 cup prepared mayonnaise

*⅓ cup spicy dark mustard,
  preferably Creole mustard*

3 tablespoons grated horseradish

4 teaspoons paprika

¾ teaspoon cayenne

*4 green onions, finely chopped
  (white & tender green parts)*

¼ cup finely chopped celery

¼ cup minced fresh parsley

Shrimp Salad:

*1½ pounds cooked medium
  shrimp, peeled & deveined*

4 cups shredded iceberg lettuce

*Lemon wedges, for garnish
  (optional)*

Prepare the sauce: In a medium-size bowl, whisk together the mayonnaise, mustard, horseradish, paprika, and cayenne until smooth. Stir in the green onions, celery, and parsley. Cover with plastic wrap and chill for at least 2 hours to allow the flavors to blend.

Prepare the salad: In a large bowl, toss the shrimp with enough sauce to coat. Cover the bowl with plastic wrap and chill for at least 3 hours or overnight.

Distribute the lettuce on 4 plates. Arrange the shrimp over the lettuce. Garnish with lemon wedges, if desired, and serve with extra sauce. **Serves 6 to 8.**

Oysters Bienville

In this rich creation the oysters are baked on a bed of rock salt, which steadies the shells and transmits heat, keeping the shells piping hot.

Bienville Sauce:

¼ cup (½ stick) butter

8 green onions, finely chopped (white & tender green parts)

½ cup finely chopped mushrooms

½ cup finely chopped green bell pepper

1 garlic clove, minced

2 tablespoons all-purpose flour

½ cup dry white wine

¼ cup oyster liquor, bottled clam juice, water, or a combination

1 large egg yolk

½ teaspoon white pepper

½ teaspoon salt

2 dozen oysters

Rock salt

2 tablespoons fine bread crumbs

2 tablespoons grated Parmesan cheese

Prepare the sauce: In a medium-size heavy skillet, melt the butter over medium heat. Add the green onions, mushrooms, bell pepper, and garlic and cook over medium-low heat, stirring frequently, for 10 minutes, or until the vegetables are very soft. Sprinkle the flour over the vegetables and cook, stirring frequently, for 2 minutes. Add the wine and oyster liquor and cook, stirring constantly, for 2 minutes, or until the sauce is smooth and bubbly.

In a small bowl, lightly beat the egg yolk. Whisk about ¼ cup of the hot sauce into the egg yolk to temper it. Return this mixture to the saucepan. Cook over low heat, stirring frequently, for 5 minutes, or until thickened slightly; do not boil. Season with the white pepper and salt. Remove the pan from the heat and set aside.

Wrought-iron balconies, French Quarter, New Orleans

Prepare the oysters: Preheat the oven to 400°F. Shuck each oyster by holding the side of the shell in a towel to prevent slippage. Insert the point of an oyster knife into the hinge of the shell, push it in, and twist to pop open. Slide the knife under the flesh to sever the bottom muscle. Discard the upper shells. In a shallow baking pan, make a bed of rock salt at least 1½ inches deep. Nestle the oysters in their bottom shells in the rock salt and spoon some of the sauce over each.

In a small bowl, combine the bread crumbs and Parmesan cheese and sprinkle over the oysters. Bake for 10 to 15 minutes, or until the crumbs are browned and the sauce is slightly bubbly. Transfer the oysters in their shells to individual plates and serve warm. **Serves 4 to 6.**

Oysters Rockefeller

So named because the topping for these baked oysters is
"as rich as Rockefeller," this sumptuous dish was invented by Jules Alciatore,
the second-generation proprietor of Antoine's Restaurant in New Orleans.
This recipe is an adaptation from *The 100 Greatest Dishes of Louisiana Cookery*
by Roy F. Guste, Jr., a direct descendant of Antoine and Jules, who claims
his recipe is very close to the original. To ensure a smooth sauce, peel the celery
with a vegetable peeler to remove the strings and fiber.

Rockefeller Sauce:

¼ cup (½ stick) butter

¼ cup all-purpose flour

1 cup shellfish stock or bottled clam
juice, including any oyster liquor

12 green onions, finely chopped
(white & tender green parts)

1½ cups minced fresh parsley
(do not include stems)

2 stalks celery, peeled
& finely chopped

1 tablespoon tomato paste

1 tablespoon sugar

2 teaspoons tarragon vinegar

½ teaspoon salt

½ teaspoon white pepper

¼ teaspoon cayenne

½ cup fine dry bread crumbs

2 dozen oysters

Rock salt

Prepare the sauce: In a medium-size heavy saucepan, melt the butter over medium heat. Add the flour and cook, stirring constantly, for 1 minute; do not brown. Whisk in the shellfish stock and cook, stirring occasionally, for 2 minutes, or until smooth and bubbly.

Add the green onions, parsley, celery, tomato paste, sugar, vinegar, salt, white pepper, and cayenne. Cover tightly and cook over very low heat for 1 hour, stirring about every 10 minutes. Stir in the bread crumbs. (The sauce should be thick enough to stay on top

of the oysters when it is spooned over them. If it is not thick enough, simmer it uncovered for a few minutes. If it is too thick, add a tablespoon or so of water.)

Prepare the oysters: Preheat the oven to 400°F. Shuck the oysters (see page 15). In a large shallow baking pan, make a bed of rock salt at least 1½ inches deep. Nestle the oysters in their bottom shells in it and spoon the sauce over them. Bake for 10 to 12 minutes, or until the sauce is slightly bubbly and begins to brown.

Transfer the oysters to individual plates and serve warm. **Serves 4 to 6.**

Peppery Cheese Straws

A popular hors d'oeuvre for home entertaining in south Louisiana, these rich and flaky breadsticks are perfect with cocktails. They can also be served as an accompaniment to soups and salads.

1 cup all-purpose flour

¾ teaspoon baking powder

¾ teaspoon salt

½ teaspoon cayenne

¼ teaspoon black pepper

6 tablespoons unsalted butter, chilled & cut into small pieces

1 cup shredded sharp cheddar cheese

3 tablespoons grated Parmesan cheese

In a small bowl, whisk together the flour, baking powder, salt, cayenne, and black pepper.

In a food processor fitted with the metal blade, combine the butter, cheddar, and Parmesan and process until smooth. Add the flour mixture and process by pulsing on and off until the dough begins to gather into a ball. Scrape the dough from the workbowl, shape it into a ball, and flatten into a disk. Wrap with plastic and chill for at least 30 minutes, or up to 2 days.

Preheat the oven to 325°F. Divide the dough in half. Chill one half while working with the other. Roll out the dough on a lightly floured work surface to ⅛ inch thick. Cut the dough into strips approximately 8 inches long and ½ inch wide. Transfer the strips to an ungreased baking sheet, spacing them about 1½ inches apart. Bake for 12 to 16 minutes, or until light golden brown. Repeat with the remaining dough.

Set the baking sheet on a wire rack and allow the cheese straws to cool. Serve them the same day they are baked. **Makes about 3 dozen breadsticks.**

Muffaletta

The Central Grocery, an emporium of imported foods across from the French Market, is the most famous purveyor of muffalettas in the city. This round sesame loaf, layered with meats and cheeses and topped with olive salad ~ the one essential ingredient ~ reflects the Italian influence on New Orleans cooking.

Olive Salad:

1 (3-ounce) jar pimiento-stuffed green olives, drained and sliced (1 cup)

1 stalk celery, thinly sliced

1 large tomato, seeded & coarsely chopped

1 garlic clove, minced

¼ cup olive oil

1 tablespoon red wine vinegar

1 teaspoon dried oregano

¼ teaspoon black pepper

1 round loaf sesame seed Italian bread, 9 to 10 inches in diameter

2 ounces thinly sliced baked ham

2 ounces thinly sliced Genoa salami

2 ounces thinly sliced provolone cheese

2 ounces thinly sliced mozzarella cheese

Prepare the olive salad: Place the olives in a strainer and rinse with cold water; drain well. In a medium-size bowl, combine the olives with the remaining salad ingredients and mix well; cover with plastic wrap and chill until ready to use.

To assemble the muffaletta, split the loaf of bread in half. Layer the bottom half with the ham, salami, provolone, and mozzarella. Spread the olive salad over the cheese and cover with the top piece of bread. Cut the sandwich into quarters. **Serves 4.**

Cajun Corn Bread

In Cajun country, cooks prefer to bake their corn bread in
cast iron ~ a square pan, skillet, or cornstick pan ~ which they preheat
so the finished bread has a deliciously crispy outside crust. If you
don't have cast iron, use a 9-inch square baking pan but don't preheat it.

*¼ cup bacon drippings
or vegetable oil*

*1 cup yellow cornmeal,
preferably stone-ground*

1 cup all-purpose flour

1 tablespoon baking powder

1 tablespoon sugar

¾ teaspoon salt

2 large eggs

¼ cup finely chopped onion

*3 fresh or pickled jalapeño
peppers, seeded & finely
chopped*

1 cup milk

Preheat the oven to 425°F. Use 1 tablespoon of the bacon drippings to grease a 9-inch cast-iron skillet or square baking pan. Set the pan over low heat to preheat while you make the batter.

In a medium-size bowl, whisk together the cornmeal, flour, baking powder, sugar, and salt.

In another medium-size bowl, combine the remaining bacon drippings, eggs, onion, jalapeños, and milk. Add to the cornmeal mixture, stirring until just combined. (Do not overbeat or the corn bread will be tough.) Test the pan by dropping in a small amount of batter; if the pan is hot enough, the batter will sizzle slightly. Pour the batter into the pan and bake in the center of the oven for 15 to 22 minutes, or until the top is golden brown and a toothpick inserted into the center comes out clean.

Cut the corn bread into 12 rectangles or wedges and serve warm. **Serves 6 to 9.**

Oyster Po'boy

The po'boy (or poor boy) is New Orleans' answer to the hoagie, hero, and submarine sandwich. The more overstuffed and juicier the sandwich, the better, so serve it with lots of napkins!

½ cup prepared mayonnaise

1 teaspoon grated lemon zest

1 tablespoon fresh lemon juice

⅔ cup yellow cornmeal

½ teaspoon cayenne

½ teaspoon black pepper

½ teaspoon salt

2 dozen shucked oysters, drained & patted dry

Vegetable oil, for frying

4 French bread rolls, 3 to 4 ounces each

3 cups shredded lettuce

2 large tomatoes, thinly sliced

In a small bowl, combine the mayonnaise, lemon zest, and lemon juice until well blended; cover with plastic wrap and chill until ready to use.

In a shallow dish, combine the cornmeal, cayenne, black pepper, and salt. Roll the oysters in the cornmeal mixture to coat completely.

In a large heavy skillet, preferably cast iron, heat ½ inch of oil over medium heat to 350°F, or until hot but not smoking. (If a cube of bread browns in about 20 seconds, the oil is ready.)

Add half the oysters and cook, turning carefully with tongs, for about 3 minutes, or until the coating is golden brown. Remove with a slotted spoon to paper towels to drain. Repeat with the remaining oysters.

Split the rolls lengthwise and pull out the inner bread to make a pocket for the oysters; spread with the mayonnaise mixture. Place the fried oysters in the bread and top with shredded lettuce and tomatoes. Cover each po'boy with the top of a roll. **Serves 4.**

Beignets

Beignets are sweet little pillows of puffed fried dough dusted with powdered sugar. They are the specialty of Café du Monde, located in the New Orleans French Market, and make a delicious snack, especially when accompanied by a cup of steaming café au lait.

1¼ cups all-purpose flour
1½ teaspoons baking powder
½ teaspoon salt
¼ teaspoon mace
1 large egg

1 tablespoon granulated sugar
½ cup milk
½ teaspoon vanilla extract
Vegetable oil, for frying
Confectioners' sugar, for dusting

In a medium-size bowl, whisk together the flour, baking powder, salt, and mace.

In a small bowl, whisk together the egg, granulated sugar, milk, and vanilla. Add to the flour mixture, stirring until a soft dough forms. (If the dough is too sticky to roll out, add 1 to 2 tablespoons additional flour.)

On a floured work surface, knead the dough for 15 seconds, or until just smooth. Roll out to ½-inch thickness and, using a floured knife, cut into about twenty-four 1½- to 2-inch squares.

In a large heavy skillet, preferably cast iron, heat ½ inch of oil over medium heat to 350°F, or until hot but not smoking. (If a cube of bread browns in 20 seconds, the oil is ready.)

Carefully drop half the squares of dough into the oil. Cook, turning once or twice with a fork, for 2 minutes, or until puffed and golden. Remove with a slotted spoon to paper towels to drain.

While still hot, sprinkle the beignets with confectioners' sugar. Repeat with the remaining dough. Serve warm. **Makes about 2 dozen beignets.**

Pain Perdu

Pain perdu ("lost bread" in French) is another example
of how Creole cooks can transform an otherwise useless ingredient ~ in this
case stale French bread ~ into a classic dish. The bread is "lost" only in
the sense that it is temporarily invisible while it is saturated in the egg mixture.
Serve this dish with the syrup or preserve of your choice.

3 large eggs
2 tablespoons granulated sugar
1 cup milk
1 teaspoon vanilla extract
¼ teaspoon cinnamon

5 tablespoons butter
8 slices day-old French bread,
  ¾ inch thick
Confectioners' sugar, for dusting
Fresh strawberries (optional)

Preheat the oven to 200°F. In a medium-size bowl, whisk together the eggs and granulated sugar until well blended. Whisk in the milk, vanilla, and cinnamon.

In a large skillet, melt 2½ tablespoons of the butter over medium heat. Dip 4 slices of bread in the egg mixture, letting it soak for a few seconds so the bread is saturated but not falling apart.

Transfer the bread to the skillet and cook over medium to medium-low heat, turning once, for 4 to 5 minutes, or until golden brown on both sides. Using a spatula, transfer the bread to a plate and keep warm in the oven. Add the rest of the butter to the skillet and repeat with the remaining bread and egg mixture.

Sprinkle lightly with confectioners' sugar and serve warm with fresh strawberries, if desired. **Serves 4.**

Omelets with Andouille Creole Sauce

If you can't find andouille, use kielbasa or another
smoked sausage and add a pinch of cayenne for spiciness.

Andouille Creole Sauce:

¼ pound andouille or other spicy
smoked sausage such as
kielbasa, cut into ¼-inch slices

1 tablespoon butter

1 small onion, chopped

½ cup seeded & chopped green
bell pepper

1 small garlic clove, minced

2 medium tomatoes, peeled,
seeded, & chopped

¼ teaspoon sugar

¼ teaspoon dried thyme

⅛ teaspoon black pepper

Omelets:

5 large eggs, at room temperature

½ teaspoon salt

¼ teaspoon black pepper

¼ teaspoon hot-pepper sauce

2 teaspoons butter

Minced fresh parsley, for garnish
(optional)

Prepare the sauce: In a large skillet, cook the andouille over medium heat, stirring frequently, for 6 minutes, or until lightly browned and some fat is rendered. Remove the sausage with a slotted spoon to paper towels to drain; do not wipe the skillet clean.

Melt the butter in the skillet over medium heat. Add the onion, bell pepper, and garlic, and cook, stirring occasionally, for 5 minutes, or until the vegetables begin to soften. Add the tomatoes, sugar, thyme, and black pepper. Cook, uncovered, for about 5 minutes, or until most but not all of the liquid has evaporated. Return the andouille to the skillet and cook, stirring occasionally, for 3 to 5 minutes, or until heated through. Keep warm.

Prepare the omelets: In a medium-size bowl, whisk together the eggs, salt, black pepper, and hot-pepper sauce. In an 8-inch omelet pan, melt 1 teaspoon of butter over medium heat until it begins to foam. Pour half the egg mixture into the pan. As the bottom begins to set, use a spatula to lift up the edges of the egg to let the uncooked portion run underneath. When the omelet is almost set, fold it in thirds, then slide onto a warm plate. Keep warm. Wipe out the pan and repeat with the remaining butter and egg.

To serve, spoon the warm sauce over the omelets and sprinkle with parsley, if desired. **Serves 2**.

Eggs Benedict

This popular brunch dish originated at the legendary Delmonico's in New York City but has since become closely associated with brunch at Brennan's Restaurant in New Orleans.

Hollandaise Sauce:

3 large egg yolks

2 tablespoons fresh lemon juice

¾ cup (1½ sticks) butter, melted

3 tablespoons hot water

½ teaspoon salt

⅛ teaspoon cayenne

4 English muffins, split

3 tablespoons butter

8 slices Canadian bacon

Poached Eggs:

1 tablespoon white vinegar

½ teaspoon salt

8 large eggs, at room temperature

Paprika, for garnish

Sliced black olives, for garnish

Prepare the sauce: In a medium-size stainless steel bowl, combine the egg yolks and lemon juice and whisk until light and frothy. Set the bowl over a medium-size saucepan of barely simmering (not boiling) water. Gradually add the melted butter and cook, whisking constantly, for 3 minutes, or until the sauce has thickened slightly. Whisk in the hot water. Remove the pan from the heat. Stir in the salt and cayenne. Set the bowl over warm water to keep warm. (Hollandaise can be held up to 45 minutes.) (Makes about 1 cup.)

Toast the English muffins until pale golden and spread each with ½ to 1 teaspoon of butter. Keep warm.

In a large skillet, melt the remaining butter over medium heat. Add the bacon and cook, turning once, for 5 minutes, or until brown around

the edges. Remove to paper towels to drain.

Prepare the eggs: Fill a large skillet two thirds full of water. Add the vinegar and salt and bring to a simmer over medium heat. Break each egg into a small cup and slip it gently into the simmering water. (This may need to be done in two batches.) Spoon the simmering water over the eggs until the egg whites are set, about 3 minutes. Carefully remove with a slot-ted spoon and drain on paper towels.

To serve, place 1 or 2 muffin halves on each plate. Top with a slice of bacon, then a poached egg. Spoon a ribbon of warm hollandaise sauce over the egg, sprinkle with paprika, and top with olive slices. **Serves 4 to 8.**

Redfish Courtbouillon

In French cooking, *court bouillon* is a vegetable broth used for poaching fish. In Louisiana it has been transformed into a rich and satisfying spicy stew.

¼ cup vegetable oil

¼ cup all-purpose flour

1 medium onion, chopped

1 medium green bell pepper, seeded & chopped

1 stalk celery, chopped

4 green onions, thinly sliced (white & tender green parts)

2 garlic cloves, minced

½ cup dry white or dry red wine

1 cup fish stock or bottled clam juice

1 (16-ounce) can whole tomatoes, in juice

1 tablespoon fresh lemon juice

2 bay leaves

½ teaspoon cayenne

½ teaspoon dried thyme

Salt & black pepper

6 redfish fillets, 4 to 6 ounces each

Green onions, for garnish

In a large heavy skillet, heat the oil over medium heat. Add the flour and cook, stirring constantly, for 3 minutes, or until a pale golden color. Add the onion, bell pepper, celery, green onions, and garlic, and cook, stirring frequently, for 5 minutes, or until softened.

Add the wine, fish stock, and tomatoes with their juice. Use the side of a spoon to break up the tomatoes. Stir in the lemon juice, bay leaves, cayenne, and thyme. Season to taste with salt and black pepper. Reduce the heat to low and cook, partially covered, for 25 to 30 minutes, or until the sauce has thickened.

Place the fillets in the sauce and cook, covered, over low heat for 5 to 8 minutes, or until the fish is opaque and flaky. Garnish with green onions and serve. **Serves 6.**

Louisiana Jambalaya

This dish had humble beginnings as a poor man's
catchall for leftover meats, fish, and sausages and plenty of rice.
Today it is one of the most revered dishes in Louisiana,
and both Creole and Cajun cuisines proudly claim it as their own.

2 pounds chicken parts

½ teaspoon cayenne

2 tablespoons vegetable oil

*8 ounces andouille or other spicy
smoked sausage such as
kielbasa, cut into ¼-inch slices*

1 medium onion, chopped

*1 medium green bell pepper,
seeded & chopped*

1 stalk celery, sliced

2 garlic cloves, minced

1 teaspoon dried thyme

1 cup long-grain rice

*1 (16-ounce) can whole
tomatoes, in juice*

*1 cup fish stock or bottled
clam juice*

½ to 1 cup water

1 bay leaf

*½ pound shrimp with tails,
shelled & deveined*

*4 green onions, thinly sliced
(white & tender green parts)*

*½ teaspoon hot-pepper sauce,
or to taste*

Pat the chicken dry, then sprinkle on all sides with the cayenne.

In a large heavy saucepan or Dutch oven, heat the oil over medium-high heat. Add the chicken and cook for 4 minutes on each side, or until browned. Add the sausage and cook, stirring occasionally, for about 3 minutes, or until it begins to brown. Remove the chicken and sausage with a slotted spoon to a plate.

Add the onion, bell pepper, celery, and garlic to the skillet and cook, stirring frequently, for 4 minutes, or until the vegetables begin

to soften. Add the thyme and rice and cook, stirring frequently, for 1 minute, or until the rice is coated with oil. Add the tomatoes with their juice, breaking them up with the side of a spoon. Stir in the fish stock, ½ cup water, and the bay leaf.

Return the chicken and sausage to the skillet. Bring the mixture to a simmer over medium-high heat. Reduce the heat to low and cook, covered, for 15 minutes. Distribute the shrimp over the top, pressing them lightly into the rice. Cook, covered, for 15 minutes more, or until the chicken and shrimp are cooked through and the rice is tender. (If the rice has absorbed all of the liquid before it is tender, add up to ½ cup more water and cook for a few minutes longer.) Remove the skillet from the heat.

Stir in the green onions and season to taste with the hot-pepper sauce. **Serves 4.**

Pasta with Cajun Ham and Oysters

This recipe is an adaptation from *Patout's Cajun Home Cooking* by
Alex Patout, and is similar to the fabulous pasta dish served in his restaurant on
Royal Street in the French Quarter. This recipe calls for tasso, a very
spicy smoked Cajun ham, but any good-quality smoked ham can be substituted.

¼ cup (½ stick) butter

6 ounces tasso or other smoked
  ham, cut into small cubes

1½ cups heavy cream

¾ teaspoon dried thyme

½ teaspoon dried basil

¼ teaspoon cayenne

¼ teaspoon black pepper

¼ teaspoon white pepper

1½ dozen small shucked oysters,
  with their liquor

8 green onions, thinly sliced
  (white & tender green parts)

1 pound dried spaghetti

In a large skillet, melt the butter over medium heat. Add the ham and cook, stirring frequently, for 3 to 4 minutes, or until the ham is tinged a deep golden brown. Add the cream, thyme, basil, cayenne, and black and white pepper and cook, stirring occasionally, over medium-low heat, for 3 minutes, or until the sauce has slightly thickened. Add the oyster liquor and cook, stirring occasionally, for 3 minutes. Add the oysters and green onions and cook, stirring occasionally, for 2 minutes, or until the edges of the oysters begin to curl. Remove the skillet from the heat and keep warm.

Bring a large saucepan of salted water to a boil over high heat. Cook the spaghetti in boiling water for 8 to 10 minutes, or until al dente; drain in a colander.

To serve, transfer the pasta to individual serving plates. Spoon the sauce over the spaghetti. **Serves 4.**

Seafood Filé Gumbo

This gumbo is flavored and thickened with filé powder rather than okra. Filé, one of the Choctaw Indians' gifts to Louisiana bayou cuisine, is made from dried and ground sassafras leaves and has a distinctive flavor reminiscent of dried thyme. Be sure to add the filé after the pan has been removed from the heat, because extra cooking can make it tough and ropy.

¼ cup vegetable oil

¼ cup all-purpose flour

1 large onion, chopped

1 medium green bell pepper, seeded & chopped

2 stalks celery, chopped

6 green onions, thinly sliced (white & tender green parts)

2 garlic cloves, minced

6 cups water

2 cups shrimp stock or bottled clam juice

¼ cup minced fresh parsley

½ teaspoon cayenne

1 pound medium shrimp, shelled & deveined

½ pound fresh crabmeat, picked over

1½ dozen shucked oysters, with their liquor

1½ tablespoons filé powder

Salt & black pepper

3 cups hot cooked white rice

In a large heavy saucepan or Dutch oven, heat the oil over medium heat. Sprinkle the flour over the oil and cook over medium to medium-high heat, stirring constantly, for 6 to 10 minutes, or until the mixture (roux) turns a deep reddish brown. (Watch carefully to prevent burning.) Add the onion, bell pepper, celery, green onions, and garlic, and cook, stirring frequently, for 5 minutes, or until the vegetables begin to soften. Stir in the water, shrimp stock, parsley, and cayenne. Cook, partially covered, over low heat for 25 minutes.

Add the shrimp, crabmeat, and oysters. Cook, uncovered, over medium-low heat, for 5 minutes, or until the shrimp turn pink and the oysters begin to curl around the edges. Remove the pan from the heat and stir in the filé powder. Season to taste with salt and pepper.

To serve, spoon about ½ cup of hot rice into soup bowls or onto serving plates and spoon the gumbo over the rice. **Serves 6.**

Gumbo Z'Herbes

It is said that this meatless gumbo, which is often served on
Good Friday, brings friendship and good luck in the coming year, and that for every
green that is added to it, a new friend will be made. This version uses
convenient (and usually very good quality) frozen greens. If you are able to get fresh
greens, use about 1½ pounds to replace each package of frozen.

¼ cup (½ stick) butter

¼ cup all-purpose flour

1 large onion, chopped

1 medium green bell pepper,
   seeded & chopped

2 stalks celery, chopped

8 green onions, thinly sliced
   (white & tender green parts)

4 garlic cloves, minced

10 cups water or vegetable stock

2 (10-ounce) packages frozen
   collard, turnip, or mustard
   greens, thawed

1 (10-ounce) package
   frozen spinach leaves, thawed

4 cups shredded green cabbage

2 bay leaves

1 teaspoon dried basil

1 teaspoon dried thyme

¼ teaspoon allspice

¼ teaspoon grated nutmeg

⅛ teaspoon ground cloves

1 tablespoon sugar

½ cup minced fresh parsley

1½ dozen shucked oysters, with
   their liquor (optional)

2 tablespoons filé powder

½ teaspoon hot-pepper sauce,
   or to taste

Salt & black pepper

4 cups hot cooked white rice

In a large heavy saucepan or Dutch oven, melt
the butter over medium heat. Sprinkle the flour
over the butter and cook over medium to

medium-high heat, stirring constantly, for 6
to 10 minutes, or until the mixture (roux) turns
a medium-dark reddish brown. (Watch

Freshwater swamp in autumn

carefully to prevent burning.) Add the onion, bell pepper, celery, green onions, and garlic, and cook, stirring frequently, for 5 minutes, or until the vegetables begin to soften. Stir in the water, greens, spinach, cabbage, bay leaves, basil, thyme, allspice, nutmeg, cloves, and sugar. Bring the mixture to a boil over medium-high heat. Reduce the heat to low and cook, partially covered, for 30 minutes.

Add the parsley and the oysters with their liquor, if desired. Cook, uncovered, for 5 minutes, or until the edges of the oysters begin to curl. Remove the pan from the heat and stir in the filé powder. Season to taste with hot-pepper sauce, salt, and black pepper.

To serve, spoon about ½ cup of hot rice into the bottom of each soup bowl and ladle the gumbo on top. **Serves 8.**

Chicken, Andouille, and Okra Gumbo

The best known of all Louisiana dishes, gumbo incorporates a French roux base, Spanish peppers, African okra (the word gumbo is derived from the African word for okra), and, in this case, spicy Cajun sausage (andouille).

6 chicken thighs
(about 2 pounds)

½ teaspoon black pepper

5 to 6 tablespoons vegetable oil

¾ pound andouille or other spicy
smoked sausage such as
kielbasa, cut into ½-inch slices

⅓ cup all-purpose flour

1 large onion, chopped

1 large green bell pepper,
seeded & chopped

6 green onions, thinly sliced
(white & tender green parts)

2 stalks celery, chopped

1½ cups okra, cut into ¼-inch
slices, or 1 (10-ounce) package
frozen sliced okra, thawed

4 cups chicken stock

6 cups water

1 teaspoon dried thyme

2 bay leaves

½ teaspoon cayenne

¼ teaspoon hot-pepper sauce

Salt

3 cups hot cooked white rice

Pat the chicken dry, then sprinkle with the black pepper. Set aside.

In a large heavy saucepan or Dutch oven, heat 2 tablespoons of the oil over medium heat. Add the sausage and cook, stirring frequently, for 3 to 5 minutes, or until browned on both sides. Remove to paper towels to drain.

Add the chicken to the pan and cook, turning once or twice, for 6 minutes, or until browned on both sides. Remove with tongs to a plate.

Using a measuring spoon, measure the pan drippings, then add enough oil to the pan to make a total of 5 tablespoons. Sprinkle the

French Quarter, New Orleans

flour over the oil and cook over medium to medium-high heat, stirring constantly, for 6 to 10 minutes, or until the mixture (roux) turns a deep reddish brown. (Watch carefully to prevent burning.) Add the onion, bell pepper, green onions, and celery and cook over medium heat, stirring frequently, for 5 minutes, or until the vegetables begin to soften. Stir in the okra, chicken stock, and water. Return the sausage and the chicken to the pan and add the thyme, bay leaves, and cayenne. Cook, partially covered, over low heat for about 30 minutes, or until the chicken is cooked through and tender.

Remove the chicken with a slotted spoon to a plate. When cool enough to handle, remove the meat, discarding the skin and bones. Cut the chicken into bite-size pieces and return it to the gumbo. (The gumbo should be the consistency of a moderately thick soup. If too thick, add a little additional water. If too thin, simmer, uncovered, for a few minutes longer.) Season to taste with the hot-pepper sauce and salt.

To serve, spoon about ½ cup of hot rice into soup bowls and spoon the gumbo over the rice. **Serves 6.**

Red Beans and Rice

This dish is traditionally served on Monday ~ which used to be wash day ~ because the beans and ham bone could simmer all day while the laundry was being done.

1½ cups (about 12 ounces) dried red beans or kidney beans, rinsed

1 ham hock or meaty ham bone (optional)

¾ teaspoon salt

1 tablespoon vegetable oil

12 ounces andouille or other spicy smoked sausage such as kielbasa, cut into ½-inch slices

1 large onion, chopped

1 medium green bell pepper, seeded & chopped

1 stalk celery, chopped

4 green onions, thinly sliced (white & tender green parts)

2 bay leaves

¼ teaspoon black pepper

½ teaspoon dried thyme

½ teaspoon hot-pepper sauce, or to taste

Rice:

3 cups water

1½ cups long-grain rice

½ teaspoon salt

In a large saucepan, cover the beans in cold water and soak for 8 hours or overnight. To quick-soak the beans, bring the water and beans to a boil, uncovered, for 2 minutes. Remove the pan from the heat, cover, and let stand for 1 hour.

Drain the beans, rinse the pan, then return the beans to the pan. Cover the beans with 6 cups of fresh cold water. Add the ham hock, if desired. Bring the mixture to a simmer over medium-high heat. Reduce the heat to low and cook, covered, for 1 to 1½ hours, stirring occasionally, or until the beans are almost tender. Stir in the salt.

Remove the ham hock with tongs to a cutting board. Cut any meat off the ham bone, add it to the pan, and discard the bone.

In a large skillet, heat the oil over medium heat. Add the sausage and cook, stirring frequently, for 5 minutes, or until it begins to brown. Add the onion, bell pepper, celery, and green onions. Cook, stirring frequently, for 5 minutes, or until the vegetables begin to soften. Add the sausage mixture to the pan with the beans.

Add the bay leaves, black pepper, and thyme to the beans and continue cooking, uncovered, over low heat, for 30 to 45 minutes, or until the beans are very tender.

Meanwhile, prepare the rice: In a medium-size saucepan, bring the water to a boil over high heat. Add the rice and salt and cook, covered, over low heat for 20 minutes, or until the rice is tender and the liquid is absorbed.

Using the back of a large spoon, mash about one quarter of the beans against the side of the pan to thicken the mixture. Season to taste with the hot-pepper sauce. Remove the pan from the heat and keep warm.

To serve, divide the rice among 6 individual shallow bowls or plates and spoon the beans over the rice. **Serves 6**.

Shrimp Creole

Spicy, hot, and full of flavor, the sauce for this dish incorporates
the Creole "holy trinity" of vegetables ~ onions, bell peppers, and tomatoes.

2 tablespoons butter

1 large onion, chopped

1 large green bell pepper,
    seeded & chopped

1 stalk celery, sliced

2 garlic cloves, minced

4 large tomatoes (about 2
    pounds), peeled, seeded
    & coarsely chopped, or 1 large
    (28-ounce) can whole tomatoes,
    drained & coarsely chopped

1 cup shrimp stock or
    bottled clam juice

½ teaspoon paprika

½ teaspoon salt

½ teaspoon dried thyme

¼ teaspoon cayenne

¼ teaspoon black pepper

1 bay leaf

1 pound large shrimp,
    peeled & deveined

3 cups hot cooked white rice

4 green onions, thinly sliced
    (white & tender green parts),
    for garnish

In a large skillet or saucepan, melt the butter over medium heat. Add the onion, bell pepper, celery, and garlic and cook, stirring frequently, for 5 minutes, or until the vegetables begin to soften. Add the tomatoes, shrimp stock, paprika, salt, thyme, cayenne, black pepper, and bay leaf. Reduce the heat to low and cook, stirring occasionally, for 25 minutes, or until the sauce is quite thick.

Add the shrimp and cook, stirring occasionally, for 4 minutes, or until the shrimp turn pink and are opaque.

To serve, spoon the shrimp and sauce over the hot rice and sprinkle with the sliced green onions. **Serves 4**.

Barbecued Shrimp

There are many variations of this recipe ~ none of which calls for a barbecue grill! The name comes from its lip-searing spicy sauce. In New Orleans, where there is an abundance of fresh shrimp, the dish is usually made with whole shrimp (head and tail intact). If you can't find them this way, make sure to use shrimp in their shells; the meat picks up too much spice when it cooks in the sauce. Peel the cooked shrimp with your hands, dunk them in the sauce, mop up extra sauce with pieces of French bread, and pass the paper napkins!

1 cup (2 sticks) butter

2 tablespoons black pepper

2½ teaspoons dried rosemary, crumbled

1½ teaspoons paprika

1½ teaspoons salt

½ teaspoon cayenne

2 cups beer

1 tablespoon fresh lemon juice

1½ teaspoons Worcestershire sauce

2 pounds medium or large shrimp, in their shells

French bread

In a large skillet or saucepan, combine the butter, black pepper, rosemary, paprika, salt, and cayenne. Cook over medium heat, stirring frequently, until the butter melts. Add the beer and simmer, uncovered, for about 15 minutes, or until the liquid is slightly reduced. Stir in the lemon juice and Worcestershire sauce.

Add the shrimp to the sauce, stirring to coat well. Cook over medium heat, stirring occasionally, for 5 minutes, or until the shrimp turn pink and are cooked through.

To serve, transfer the shrimp and sauce to a large serving platter or spoon the shrimp into individual shallow bowls and serve the sauce on the side. Serve with French bread. **Serves 6.**

Crawfish Etouffée

If you're using fresh crawfish tails in this recipe, save any of the orange fat extracted from the heads and tops of the tails and add it to the sauce for extra flavor.

Roux Base:

¼ cup vegetable oil

6 tablespoons all-purpose flour

1 large onion, chopped

1 large green bell pepper,
seeded & chopped

2 stalks celery, chopped

3 garlic cloves, finely chopped

2 cups crawfish stock or
bottled clam juice

1 teaspoon dried basil

1 teaspoon dried thyme

½ teaspoon cayenne

½ teaspoon salt, or to taste

Crawfish:

6 tablespoons butter

8 green onions, thinly sliced
(white & tender green parts)

2 pounds crawfish tails, peeled,
or 1½ pounds medium shrimp,
peeled & deveined

2 tablespoons fresh lemon juice

1 tablespoon Worcestershire sauce

½ cup minced fresh parsley

½ teaspoon hot-pepper sauce

3 cups hot cooked white rice

Prepare the roux: In a large heavy saucepan or Dutch oven, heat the oil over medium heat for 1 minute. Add the flour and cook over medium to medium-high heat, stirring constantly, for 6 to 10 minutes, or until the roux turns a rich mahogany color. (Watch carefully to prevent burning.) Add the onion, bell pepper, celery, and garlic. Cook, stirring frequently, for 4 minutes, or until the vegetables begin to soften. Whisk in the stock, bring to a boil over medium-high heat, and cook, stirring constantly, for 1 minute. Stir

in the basil, thyme, cayenne, and salt. Reduce the heat to low and cook, covered, stirring occasionally, for 10 minutes.

Prepare the crawfish: In a large skillet, melt 3 tablespoons of the butter over medium heat. Add the green onions and the crawfish tails and cook, stirring frequently, for 3 minutes, or until the crawfish turns pink. Stir in the lemon juice and Worcestershire sauce.

Add the crawfish mixture to the roux base.

Cut the remaining 3 tablespoons of butter into small pieces. Reduce the heat to very low and add the butter to the mixture, 1 piece at a time, stirring well after each addition. (The object is to produce a creamy texture.) Stir in the parsley and hot-pepper sauce.

To serve, divide the rice among 6 serving plates and spoon the mixture over the rice. **Serves 6**.

Blackened Redfish

This dish, invented by Paul Prudhomme in the early 1980s,
calls for redfish coated with a mixture of herbs and spices, then seared in a white-
hot skillet. This delicious cooking method works for any firm-fleshed fish,
such as pompano, black drum, red snapper, trout, and salmon. Be sure the stove burner
is under a good vent because the cooking process can create some smoke.

1 teaspoon paprika

1 teaspoon black pepper

1 teaspoon salt

½ teaspoon cayenne

½ teaspoon garlic powder

½ teaspoon onion powder

½ teaspoon dried oregano

½ teaspoon white pepper

½ teaspoon dried thyme

*4 redfish fillets, 6 ounces each,
cut ½ inch thick*

4 teaspoons butter, melted

In a shallow bowl, combine all the spices and herbs. Heat a large cast-iron skillet over medium-high heat for about 10 minutes, or until very hot. (The skillet is the correct temperature if a drop of water evaporates almost immediately when dropped on the surface.)

Coat the fillets with the spice mixture, shaking off the excess. Cook the fish in the preheated skillet for 2 to 3 minutes, or until the underside is dark brown. Carefully spoon about ½ teaspoon of the melted butter over each fillet (try to avoid spilling the butter into the pan because it may flare up). Using a spatula, turn the fish and spoon ½ teaspoon of the butter over the blackened sides of the fillets. Cook for 2 to 3 minutes more, or until the underside is dark brown and the fish is opaque but still moist inside. Transfer the fish to serving plates. **Serves 4.**

Pompano en Papillote

Cooking food in parchment (en papillote) is a classic French
method that enhances the flavors of the food by sealing in the juices. For this dish,
perfected in 1901 at Antoine's Restaurant in honor of the visiting
French balloonist Alberto Santos-Dumont, the parchment paper was cut in the shape
of a heart and folded in such a way that when it puffed during baking it
resembled a balloon. Pompano is plentiful in New Orleans, but almost any kind of fish,
including sole, cod, flounder, and red snapper, can be substituted.

Poached Pompano:

1 small onion, quartered

½ lemon, sliced

8 peppercorns

1 teaspoon salt

1 bay leaf, broken in half

4 pompano fillets, 5 to 6
ounces each

Seafood Sauce:

3 tablespoons butter

3 tablespoons all-purpose flour

4 green onions, thinly sliced
(white & tender green parts)

½ cup dry white wine

½ teaspoon salt, or to taste

⅛ teaspoon white pepper

½ pound small shrimp, peeled

¼ pound lump crabmeat,
picked over

Prepare the pompano: Fill a large skillet halfway with water. Add the onion, lemon, peppercorns, salt, and bay leaf. Bring the mixture to a simmer over medium heat and cook, uncovered, for 5 minutes. Add the pompano fillets and cook, uncovered, over low heat, frequently spooning some of the liquid over the fish, for 4 to 6 minutes, or until the flesh is opaque but still moist. Remove with a slotted spatula to a plate and let cool slightly. Boil the poaching liquid over high heat for 5 minutes to reduce by about half. Strain the mixture through a fine sieve and set aside 1 cup of the liquid.

Prepare the sauce: In a medium-size heavy saucepan, melt the butter over medium heat. Add the flour and cook, stirring constantly, for 2 minutes. Add the green onions and cook, stirring frequently, for 1 minute, or until softened slightly. Whisk in the reserved poaching liquid and wine, bring to a boil over medium-high heat, and cook, whisking constantly, for 1 minute. Add the salt and pepper. Stir in the shrimp and cook, stirring frequently, for 3 minutes, or until pink. Gently fold in the crabmeat. Taste and adjust seasonings if necessary. Transfer to a medium-size bowl and cool completely. (The sauce should be very thick when it is used.)

Preheat the oven to 425°F. Butter a baking sheet. Cut four hearts out of parchment paper approximately 14 inches across and 10 inches high. Lay them flat and lightly butter them. Spoon a quarter of the sauce onto one side of each heart and top each with a fillet. Fold the other side of the heart over and fold the edges of the open side to seal the pouch. Place the sealed parchment packages on the prepared baking sheet. Bake for 8 minutes, or until the paper is puffed and browned.

To serve, present each person with a sealed package. Using 2 forks, tear and fold open the bag to expose the fish and sauce. **Serves 4**.

Crab au Gratin

Here is a classic yet simple way to serve crabmeat. For the best results, use the freshest crabmeat you can find. In New Orleans, the prized blue crab is the only choice.

4 tablespoons butter

2 tablespoons all-purpose flour

2½ cups half-and-half
 or light cream

1 teaspoon salt

¼ teaspoon white pepper

Pinch of cayenne

1 teaspoon lemon juice

1 pound lump crabmeat,
 picked over

¾ cup finely ground fresh
 French bread crumbs

2 tablespoons grated Parmesan cheese

1 tablespoon minced fresh parsley

Butter a 2-quart baking dish or four 8-ounce gratin dishes. In a medium-size saucepan, melt 2 tablespoons of the butter over medium heat. Add the flour and cook, stirring constantly, for 2 minutes. Whisk in the half-and-half. Bring the mixture to a boil over medium-high heat and cook, stirring constantly, for 1 minute, or until thickened slightly. Stir in the salt, white pepper, cayenne, and lemon juice. Gently fold in the crabmeat. Transfer the mixture to the prepared dish.

In a small skillet, melt the remaining 2 tablespoons butter over medium heat. Add the bread crumbs and cook, stirring frequently, for 3 to 4 minutes, or until light golden. Remove the pan from the heat and stir in the Parmesan and parsley. Sprinkle the crumbs evenly over the gratin dish.

Preheat the broiler. Broil the gratin about 8 inches from the heat for 2 to 3 minutes, or until the top is golden brown and the crab mixture is hot and bubbly. **Serves 4.**

Cornmeal-Fried Catfish

Cloaked in a crisp, spicy-hot cornmeal crust is the way they like catfish
in New Orleans. Corn flour, or very finely ground cornmeal, is preferred for coating
the fish, but because it is not available nationwide, you can use a mixture
of cornmeal and all-purpose flour, as we do here. If you are fortunate enough to find
corn flour, simply use half a cup instead of the cornmeal mixture.

1 large egg

⅓ cup milk

¼ cup cornmeal

¼ cup all-purpose flour

¾ teaspoon salt

¾ teaspoon black pepper

¼ teaspoon cayenne

Vegetable oil, for frying

*4 catfish fillets, about 6 ounces
  each, cut ½ inch thick*

Tartar sauce (optional)

*Lemon wedges, for garnish
  (optional)*

In a shallow bowl, whisk together the egg and milk. In another shallow bowl, combine the cornmeal, flour, salt, black pepper, and cayenne.

In a large deep skillet, preferably cast iron, heat about ½ inch of oil over medium heat to 350°F, or until very hot but not smoking. (If a cube of bread browns in about 20 seconds, the oil is ready.)

Dip the fish fillets in the egg mixture, then dredge in the flour mixture. Transfer the fillets to the skillet and cook for 4 to 6 minutes, turning once, or until golden brown and crusty on both sides. Remove with a slotted spatula to paper towels to drain.

Serve the fish with tartar sauce and lemon wedges, if desired. **Serves 4.**

Cajun Meat Loaf

This spicy meat loaf is terrific with a vegetable dish like Cajun Maque Choux (page 73). If you prefer a little less spice, reduce the cayenne to ½ or ¼ teaspoon.

2 tablespoons olive oil

1 medium onion, chopped

1 medium green bell pepper, seeded & chopped

2 garlic cloves, minced

1 teaspoon dried oregano

1 teaspoon dried thyme

1 teaspoon salt

¾ teaspoon cayenne

¾ teaspoon black pepper

½ teaspoon ground cumin

½ teaspoon white pepper

1 pound ground beef

½ pound ground pork

½ pound ground veal

1 cup fresh bread crumbs

½ cup tomato sauce

1 large egg

½ cup milk

Preheat the oven to 350°F. In a large skillet, heat the oil over medium heat. Add the onion, bell pepper, garlic, oregano, and thyme and cook over medium-high heat, stirring frequently, for 5 minutes, or until the vegetables begin to soften. Stir in the salt, cayenne, black pepper, cumin, and white pepper. Remove the skillet from the heat.

In a large bowl, combine the beef, pork, and veal. Add the bread crumbs, tomato sauce, egg, and milk and blend well. Gently mix in the vegetable mixture. Pack into a 9-by-5-by-3-inch loaf pan and smooth the top.

Bake for 1 hour, or until the meat loaf is firm when pressed gently and the juices run clear when the center is pierced with a knife.

Pour off most of the juices, cut the meat loaf into slices, and serve. **Serves 6 to 8**.

Duck Sauce Piquante

Sauce piquante is so appreciated in Louisiana that a Sauce Piquante Festival, dedicated to nothing but fish, meat, poultry, and seafood made with variations of this sauce, is held annually in the town of Raceland, Louisiana. In this recipe, the rich, meaty flavor of duck holds up especially well to the spicy sauce. A generous helping of fluffy white rice is a perfect accompaniment.

6 boneless duck breasts with skin, 5 to 6 ounces each

Salt & black pepper

Sauce Piquante:

2 tablespoons vegetable oil

2 tablespoons all-purpose flour

1 medium onion, chopped

1 stalk celery, chopped

½ cup seeded & chopped green bell pepper

1 garlic clove, minced

1 (16-ounce) can whole tomatoes, in juice

1 cup chicken stock

1 small fresh or pickled jalapeño pepper, finely chopped

1 bay leaf

½ teaspoon salt

½ teaspoon dried thyme

⅛ teaspoon cayenne

⅛ teaspoon black pepper

⅛ teaspoon white pepper

2 tablespoons red wine vinegar

2 green onions, finely chopped (white & tender green parts)

Prepare the duck: Preheat the oven to 325°F. Prick the duck skin in several places with a fork, sprinkle with salt and pepper, and place on a rack, skin side up, in a shallow roasting pan. Roast, uncovered, for 1 hour, or until the skin is golden brown, most of the fat has been rendered, and the duck is cooked through.

Prepare the sauce: In a large skillet or Dutch oven, heat the oil over medium heat. Add the flour and cook over medium to medium-high

heat, stirring constantly, for 3 to 5 minutes, or until the mixture (roux) is medium to dark brown. Add the onion, celery, bell pepper, and garlic and cook over medium heat, stirring frequently, for 5 minutes, or until the vegetables begin to soften. Add the tomatoes with their juice, breaking them up with the side of a spoon. Stir in the chicken stock, jalapeño, bay leaf, salt, thyme, cayenne, black and white pepper, and vinegar. Cook, covered, over low heat, stirring occasionally, for 20 minutes.

Add the duck to the sauce and cook, partially covered, for 20 minutes. Skim off the excess fat from the top of the sauce and stir in the green onions. Adjust the seasoning if necessary. **Serves 4 to 6**.

Grillades and Grits

Grillades, a big favorite on the breakfast and brunch circuit, are similar to what the rest of America calls Swiss steak ~ pieces of top round beef or veal pounded very thin. Grillades are seared in hot oil, then simmered in a spicy roux-based Creole sauce. This recipe can also be served for dinner, with the grillades' rich, thick gravy spooned over the casserole-baked grits.

Grillades:

1½ to 2 pounds well-trimmed top round of beef

1 teaspoon black pepper

¾ teaspoon salt

3 tablespoons vegetable oil

2 tablespoons all-purpose flour

1 large onion, chopped

1 large green bell pepper, seeded & chopped

2 stalks celery, chopped

2 garlic cloves, minced

2 cups beef stock, water, or a combination of the two

1 (16-ounce) can whole tomatoes, in juice

1 teaspoon dried thyme

½ teaspoon cayenne

2 bay leaves

1 teaspoon red wine vinegar

4 green onions, thinly sliced (white & tender green parts)

Baked Grits:

6 cups water

1¼ cups quick-cooking grits (not instant)

1 teaspoon salt

½ teaspoon black pepper

½ cup milk

1 large egg

3 tablespoons butter

Prepare the grillades: Cut the meat into 1½-inch-thick slices, then cut the slices into approximately 2½-inch squares. Pound the meat between pieces of waxed paper into thin pieces about double their original size. Sprinkle the beef on both sides with the black pepper and salt.

In a large skillet, heat the oil over medium heat. Cook the meat, in 2 batches if necessary, over medium-high heat, turning once or twice, for 5 minutes, or until well-browned on both sides. Remove the meat to a plate. Sprinkle the flour into the pan drippings. Cook, stirring constantly, for 2 minutes, or until the flour is lightly browned. Add the onion, bell pepper, celery, and garlic, and cook, stirring frequently, for 5 minutes, or until the vegetables begin to soften. Add the beef stock and the tomatoes with their juice, breaking up the tomatoes with the side of a spoon. Stir in the thyme, cayenne, and bay leaves. Return the meat to the sauce. Cook, covered, over low heat for 1 to 1½ hours, stirring once or twice, or until the meat is tender. Uncover the pan during the last 15 minutes of cooking to thicken the sauce

slightly. Stir in the vinegar.

Transfer the grillades and sauce to a serving platter and sprinkle with the sliced green onions.

Prepare the grits: Preheat the oven to 350°F. In a large heavy saucepan, bring the water to a boil over high heat. Gradually stir in the grits and cook over medium heat, stirring frequently, for about 7 minutes, or until thick and creamy. Stir in the salt and black pepper.

In a small bowl, whisk together the milk and egg. Whisk some of the hot grits into the egg mixture to temper the egg. Return this mixture to the saucepan. Stir in 2 tablespoons of the butter until well blended.

Grease a 2-quart baking dish. Scrape the grits into the dish and dot with the remaining butter. Bake, uncovered, for 30 to 40 minutes, or until the top is pale golden brown and the grits are heated through.

Serve the grillades with the grits on the side. **Serves 6.**

Roast Chicken with Oyster Dressing

If you'd like to turn the flavorful chicken pan drippings into a sauce, simply spoon off the excess fat, add a cup of white wine to the drippings, and cook, stirring frequently, over medium-high heat to reduce it slightly.

Oyster Dressing:

¼ cup (½ stick) butter

1 large onion, chopped

2 stalks celery, chopped

4 green onions, finely chopped (white & tender green parts)

2 dozen shucked oysters with their liquor, chopped

2 teaspoons poultry seasoning

1 teaspoon dried thyme

¾ teaspoon black pepper

½ teaspoon cayenne

½ teaspoon salt

6 cups stale French bread cubes (¾-inch pieces)

1 cup chicken stock

¼ cup minced fresh parsley

2 large eggs, lightly beaten

Chicken:

One 5- to 6-pound roasting chicken

Salt & black pepper

1 tablespoon butter

Prepare the dressing: In a large skillet, melt the butter over medium heat. Add the onion, celery, and green onions and cook, stirring frequently, for about 10 minutes, or until quite soft. Add the oysters with their liquor and cook over medium-high heat, stirring frequently, for about 4 minutes, or until some of the liquid has evaporated.

Remove the skillet from the heat and stir in the poultry seasoning, thyme, black pepper, cayenne, and salt. Add the bread cubes, chicken stock, and parsley; toss to combine well. Stir in the eggs.

Prepare the chicken: Preheat the oven to 350°F. Loosely pack the dressing into the neck and body cavities of the chicken. Bend

the wings under the bird to hold the neck cavity closed and tie the legs together with string. Place the chicken, breast side up, on a rack in a shallow roasting pan. Sprinkle the outside with salt and black pepper and rub the skin with the butter.

Roast uncovered, basting occasionally with the pan juices, for 2 hours, or until a meat thermometer registers 185°F when inserted into the thigh or the juices run clear when the leg joint is pierced with a knife.

Remove the dressing from the chicken and transfer it to a serving bowl. Carve the bird and arrange the meat on a platter. **Serves 6 to 8**.

Smothered Chicken

In this recipe, the meat is browned, then slowly cooked over low heat
in a small amount of liquid. The results are a satisfying stew with vegetables that
are meltingly sweet and meat that is so tender it falls off the bone.

⅔ cup all-purpose flour

1 teaspoon salt

½ teaspoon cayenne

½ teaspoon black pepper

½ teaspoon white pepper

One 3- to 3½-pound chicken,
    cut into 8 pieces

3 tablespoons vegetable oil

2 medium onions, chopped

1 small green bell pepper,
    seeded & chopped

1 stalk celery, chopped

2 garlic cloves, minced

1 bay leaf

1 cup chicken stock

2 green onions, thinly sliced
    (white & tender green parts)

In a small paper bag, combine the flour, salt, cayenne, and black and white pepper. Put the chicken pieces in the bag and shake to coat.

In a Dutch oven, heat the oil over medium-high heat. Shake the excess flour from the chicken, then cook, turning once or twice, for 6 minutes, or until browned on both sides. Remove to a plate.

Add the onions, bell pepper, celery, and garlic to the pan and cook over medium heat, stirring occasionally, for 5 minutes, or until softened. Stir in the bay leaf and chicken stock. Return the chicken with any accumulated juices to the pan. Bring to a simmer, then reduce the heat to low and cook, covered, stirring once or twice, for 1½ hours, or until the chicken is very tender.

Discard the bay leaf. Tilt the pan and spoon the excess fat from the top of the sauce; stir in the green onions. **Serves 4 to 6.**

Garlic Chicken

Inspired by the famous Chicken à la Grande served at Mosca's restaurant in Waggaman, Louisiana, and the Garlic Chicken at Buster Holmes's Creole Soul Food Café in New Orleans' French Quarter, this dish is strictly for real garlic lovers. Serve it with Cajun "Dirty" Rice (page 75) and Creole Stewed Okra and Tomatoes (page 69), and follow with a slice of Sweet Potato Pie (page 78) for dessert.

*One 3- to 3½-pound chicken,
cut into 8 pieces*

Salt & black pepper

3 tablespoons olive oil

3 large garlic cloves, minced

*1 teaspoon dried rosemary,
crumbled*

1 teaspoon dried oregano

½ cup dry white wine

½ teaspoon hot-pepper sauce

½ teaspoon Worcestershire sauce

Pat the chicken dry and sprinkle with salt and pepper. In a large skillet, heat the oil over medium heat. Add the chicken and cook over medium-high heat, turning once or twice, for about 6 minutes, or until browned on both sides. Reduce the heat to low and cook, covered, for about 25 minutes, or until the chicken juices run clear when a thigh is pierced. Remove with a slotted spoon to a plate.

Add the garlic, rosemary, and oregano to the skillet and cook over medium-low heat, stirring frequently, for about 2 minutes. Add the wine and bring to a boil over high heat, stirring to scrape up any browned bits from the bottom of the pan. Gently boil the sauce for 2 to 3 minutes, or until it has thickened slightly. Stir in the hot-pepper sauce and Worcestershire sauce.

Return the chicken to the skillet and cook over low heat to warm through. Serve the chicken with the sauce spooned over it. **Serves 5 to 6.**

Creole Stewed Okra and Tomatoes

Okra, which was brought to this country by African slaves, is a popular
vegetable in the South. It not only adds flavor to many southern dishes, but also serves
to thicken the liquid in which it is cooked. When buying fresh okra, choose
small pods that are firm and brightly colored (large pods may be tough and fibrous).
This side dish is a wonderful accompaniment to roasted meats or poultry.

1 pound fresh okra

3 tablespoons butter

1 medium onion, chopped

1 garlic clove, minced

2 large tomatoes, seeded &
coarsely chopped

½ cup water

1 bay leaf

1 teaspoon sugar

½ teaspoon salt

¼ teaspoon black pepper

⅛ teaspoon cayenne

Trim the stems from the okra and cut into ½-inch slices. In a large skillet, melt the butter over medium heat. Add the okra, onion, and garlic and cook, stirring frequently, for 5 minutes, or until the onion softens.

Add the tomatoes, water, bay leaf, sugar, salt, black pepper, and cayenne. Cook, covered, over low heat for about 30 minutes, stirring occasionally, or until the okra is tender. (If the sauce is too watery, cook, uncovered, over medium-high heat for 2 to 3 minutes to thicken slightly.) **Serves 6**.

Crab-Stuffed Mirliton

Also known as vegetable pear, chayote, and christophene,
the mirliton is a pear-shaped pale-green squash grown throughout Louisiana
as well as the Caribbean and Latin America. Here, the white
pulp's mild taste combines perfectly with the delicate flavor of the crab.
Serve this dish as a main course with a tossed green salad.

3 firm but ripe mirlitons

5 tablespoons butter

1 medium onion, chopped

4 green onions, thinly sliced
  (white & tender green parts)

¼ cup finely chopped celery

1 garlic clove, minced

1 cup fresh bread crumbs

½ pound fresh crabmeat,
  picked over

¼ teaspoon hot-pepper sauce

¼ teaspoon black pepper

¼ teaspoon salt

¼ teaspoon dried thyme

1 large egg, lightly beaten

Bring a large saucepan of salted water to a boil over high heat. Cook the mirlitons in the boiling water for 20 minutes, or until tender when tested with a fork. Drain the mirlitons in a colander. When cool enough to handle, cut them in half lengthwise, discard the large center seed, and scoop out the pulp, leaving the shells intact. Coarsely chop the pulp and set aside.

Preheat the oven to 350°F. In a large skillet, melt 3 tablespoons of the butter over medium heat. Add the onion, green onions, celery, and garlic and cook, stirring frequently, for 5 minutes, or until the vegetables begin to soften. Add the chopped mirliton pulp and cook, stirring frequently, for 5 minutes more, or until most of the moisture has evaporated. Stir in ¾ cup of the bread crumbs, the crabmeat, hot-pepper sauce,

Strings of garlic in the French Market, New Orleans

black pepper, salt, and thyme. Remove the skillet from the heat. Let the mixture cool slightly and stir in the egg.

Grease a 9-by-13-inch baking dish. Arrange the mirliton shells in the baking dish and blot up any moisture in the shells with paper towels. Spoon the stuffing into the shells, sprinkle with the remaining bread crumbs, and dot with the remaining butter.

Bake, uncovered, for 30 to 35 minutes, or until the stuffing is firm and the tops are golden brown. **Serves 4 to 6**.

Cajun Maque Choux

One reason this sweet corn dish tastes so good is the
distinctive flavor that bacon drippings add to the sautéed vegetables, but using
vegetable oil or butter instead will also produce good results. Cajun Maque Choux
makes a wonderful accompaniment to fried or roast chicken.

3 tablespoons bacon drippings

1 medium onion, chopped

*1 small green bell pepper,
seeded & chopped*

*2 cups fresh or frozen sweet corn
kernels, thawed if frozen*

*2 medium ripe tomatoes,
seeded & chopped*

1 teaspoon sugar

Salt & black pepper

In a medium-size skillet, heat the bacon drippings over medium heat. Add the onion and bell pepper and cook, stirring frequently, for about 10 minutes, or until the vegetables are very soft. Add the corn, tomatoes, and sugar, and season to taste with salt and black pepper. (Use salt carefully because the bacon drippings may be salty.) Cook, covered, over low heat for about 5 minutes, or until the vegetables are heated through. **Serves 4**.

Cheese Grits

Grits, a southern staple made from dried corn, are served for breakfast with ham, sausage, and poached eggs. They can also be turned into dinnertime fare with the addition of cheese, as in this recipe. If you prefer, use the old-fashioned slow-cooking hominy grits, which take about 30 minutes to soften in hot water.

3 cups water

3 cups milk

1¼ cups quick-cooking grits
(not instant)

1 teaspoon salt

½ teaspoon black pepper

½ teaspoon butter

2 cups shredded cheddar cheese

2 large eggs

Preheat the oven to 350°F. Butter a 2-quart baking dish.

In a large heavy saucepan, bring the water and milk to a boil over medium heat. Gradually stir in the grits and cook, stirring frequently, for about 7 minutes, or until thick and creamy. Stir in the salt, pepper, butter, and 1½ cups of the cheese.

Lightly beat the eggs in a small bowl.

Whisk some of the hot grits into the eggs to temper them. Return this mixture to the saucepan and stir until blended.

Spoon the mixture into the prepared dish and sprinkle with the remaining cheese. Bake for 30 to 40 minutes, or until the top is pale and golden and the grits are heated through. **Serves 6**.

Cajun "Dirty" Rice

This dish got its name because the chicken livers and gizzards turn the
rice a slightly grayish color. Dirty rice is traditionally served with poultry, but it can
also be eaten as a main course with a green salad and crusty French bread.

8 ounces chicken livers, rinsed

6 ounces chicken gizzards, rinsed

5 tablespoons butter

1 medium onion, chopped

2 garlic cloves, minced

2 cups long-grain rice

2 cups chicken stock

2 cups water

¾ teaspoon salt

½ teaspoon black pepper

½ teaspoon cayenne

*6 green onions, thinly sliced
(white & tender green parts)*

Trim the fat from the chicken livers. Cut the gizzards into 2-inch pieces. In a food processor fitted with the metal blade, combine the chicken livers and gizzards and process until finely ground. Transfer the mixture to a plate and discard any pieces of tough membrane.

In a large heavy saucepan, melt the butter over medium heat. Add the liver mixture and onion and cook, stirring frequently, for 6 minutes, or until the meat and onions are lightly browned. Add the garlic and cook, stirring frequently, for 2 minutes. Stir in the rice. Add the chicken stock, water, salt, black pepper, and cayenne. Bring the mixture to a simmer over medium-high heat. Reduce the heat to low and cook, covered, for 20 minutes, or until the rice is tender and the liquid is absorbed. Remove the pan from the heat and stir in the green onions with a fork. **Serves 4**.

Bananas Foster

Perhaps the best-known dessert from New Orleans,
Bananas Foster was created at Brennan's Restaurant, where it is always prepared
tableside. Choose bananas that are thick and relatively straight, since the thin,
curved ones are difficult to slice and turn without breaking.

4 firm but ripe bananas
¼ cup (½ stick) unsalted butter
1 cup packed light brown sugar
½ teaspoon cinnamon

¼ cup banana-flavored liqueur
  (optional)
¼ cup golden or white rum
4 scoops vanilla ice cream

Peel the bananas and cut in half. Slice each half lengthwise into quarters.

In a large skillet, melt the butter over medium heat. Add the sugar, cinnamon, and banana liqueur, if desired, and cook, stirring frequently, for about 2 minutes, or until bubbly. Add the bananas and cook, turning once, for about 2 minutes, or until slightly softened and browned. Remove the skillet from the heat.

In a small saucepan, heat the rum over low heat. Carefully light the rum using a long fireplace match. Pour the flaming rum over the bananas and sauce. Allow the sauce to flame until it dies out, swirling the pan gently to prolong the flaming.

Scoop the ice cream into shallow dessert bowls and spoon the bananas and warm sauce on top. **Serves 4**.

Sweet Potato Pie

Similar to pumpkin pie, but with a richer flavor and sturdier texture, this dessert is well loved throughout the South. For the best color, use deep red-gold sweet potatoes or yams.

Pastry Crust:

1 cup all-purpose flour

¼ teaspoon salt

3 tablespoons unsalted butter, chilled & cut into small pieces

2 tablespoons vegetable shortening, chilled

2 to 3 tablespoons ice water

Sweet Potato Filling:

2 large eggs

¾ cup sugar

2 tablespoons unsalted butter, melted

2 tablespoons molasses

2 cups cooked mashed sweet potatoes or yams

1 teaspoon grated nutmeg

½ teaspoon cinnamon

½ teaspoon ground ginger

¼ teaspoon salt

1 teaspoon pure vanilla extract

1½ cups half-and-half

Whipped cream (optional)

Prepare the crust: In a medium-size bowl, combine the flour and salt. Using your fingertips, 2 knives, or a pastry blender, cut the butter and shortening into the flour until the mixture resembles coarse meal. Sprinkle the mixture with 2 tablespoons ice water. Mix with a fork, then add enough additional water to gather the dough into a ball. Flatten it into a disk, wrap with plastic, and chill for at least 1 hour or for up to 2 days.

Remove the dough from the refrigerator and let it stand for about 10 minutes before rolling. Roll it out on a lightly floured surface into an 11-inch round. Transfer to a 9-inch

pie pan and press it into the bottom and up the sides of the pan. Trim and flute the edges. Place in the freezer until ready to fill.

Prepare the filling: Preheat the oven to 350°F. In a medium-size bowl, whisk together the eggs, sugar, melted butter, and molasses until smooth. Stir in the mashed sweet potatoes until well blended. Stir in the spices, salt, and vanilla. Gradually stir in the half-and-half.

Pour the filling into the prepared pie shell and bake in the lower third of the oven for 55 to 60 minutes, or until a knife inserted two thirds of the way into the center comes out clean. The center should still be slightly wobbly.

Set the pie on a wire rack to cool. Serve slightly warm or at room temperature with whipped cream, if desired. **Serves 8 to 10**.

Pecan Pie

Pecan pie really does taste better in New Orleans, thanks to an abundance of fresh native pecans. These nuts have an extraordinary buttery-rich flavor that complements the sweet custard filling beautifully. Make sure they are vacuum-packed or have a current shelf date when you buy them.

1 recipe Pastry Crust (p. 78)

Pecan Filling:
3 large eggs
⅔ cup sugar
1 cup dark corn syrup
⅛ teaspoon salt

2 tablespoons unsalted butter, melted
2 teaspoons pure vanilla extract
1 cup coarsely chopped pecans
12 pecan halves

Vanilla ice cream (optional)

Prepare the crust according to the recipe and transfer to a 9-inch pie pan, pressing it into the bottom and up the sides of the pan. Trim and flute the edges of the crust and place in the freezer until ready to fill.

Prepare the filling: Preheat the oven to 350°F. In a medium-size bowl, whisk together the eggs, sugar, corn syrup, salt, melted butter, and vanilla. Stir in the chopped pecans.

Pour the filling into the prepared pie crust.

Arrange the pecan halves decoratively on top of the filling. Bake in the lower third of the oven for 55 to 65 minutes, or until a knife inserted two thirds of the way into the center comes out clean. The pie will be semifirm in the middle and quiver slightly when gently shaken.

Set the pie on a wire rack to cool. Serve slightly warm or at room temperature with a scoop of vanilla ice cream, if desired. **Serves 8 to 10**.

Bread Pudding with Whiskey Sauce

There are as many recipes for bread pudding in south
Louisiana as there are cooks. Originally a thrifty dish, created from day-old bread,
sugar, eggs, and milk, now there are souffléed and whole-wheat variations,
and recipes calling for such ingredients as pineapple, fruit cocktail, and nuts. This is
quite a basic recipe, with only raisins added for contrasting flavor.
It can be served with or without whiskey sauce.

Bread Pudding:

3 large eggs

¾ cup plus 2 teaspoons sugar

2 cups half-and-half

1 cup heavy cream

1½ tablespoons pure
  vanilla extract

½ teaspoon cinnamon

¼ teaspoon grated nutmeg

16 slices day-old French bread,
  ½ inch thick

½ cup seedless dark or
  golden raisins

Whiskey Sauce:

⅔ cup sugar

¼ cup water

¼ cup (½ stick) unsalted butter

1 large egg

¼ cup whiskey

Prepare the pudding: Preheat the oven to 325°F. Grease a shallow 2-quart baking dish. In a medium-size bowl, whisk together the eggs, ¾ cup sugar, the half-and-half, cream, vanilla, cinnamon, and nutmeg.

Arrange half the bread slices in the bottom of the prepared dish and scatter half the raisins over the bread. Layer the rest of the bread on top and scatter the remaining raisins over the bread. Pour the egg mixture evenly over the bread. Place a sheet of plastic wrap directly on the surface of the pudding and place a slightly smaller pan on the plastic wrap. Put a couple of heavy cans in the pan to weigh it down so the bread is completely immersed in the egg mixture. Set aside to soak for 15 minutes.

Remove the weights and plastic wrap. Bake the pudding in the center of the oven for 20 minutes. Sprinkle the remaining 2 teaspoons of sugar over the top of the pudding and bake for 35 to 40 minutes more, or until the top is golden brown and slightly caramelized, and a knife inserted about two thirds of the way into the center comes out clean. (The pudding will sink during cooling.)

Prepare the sauce: In a medium-size heavy saucepan, combine the sugar, water, and butter. Cook over medium heat, stirring frequently, until the sugar is dissolved and small bubbles form around the edges.

In a small bowl, lightly beat the egg. Whisk about ¼ cup of the hot sugar mixture into the egg to temper it. Return this mixture to the saucepan with the hot syrup. Cook over low heat, stirring constantly, for 1 to 2 minutes, or until the sauce thickens slightly and steam begins to rise. Remove the pan from the heat and stir in the whiskey. The sauce can be made ahead and stored at cool room temperature for several hours. To reheat, warm over low heat and whisk to return it to the right consistency. (Makes about 1¼ cups.)

To serve, spoon the bread pudding, either warm or at room temperature, into shallow dessert bowls and pour the whiskey sauce over it. **Serves 6 to 8**.

Pralines

Pralines are flat, round, pecan-studded candies. In this recipe, butter and milk are added to produce a soft, almost chewy, texture. Traditionally, these sweets are served for dessert with strong coffee.

1½ cups granulated sugar

1½ cups packed light
   brown sugar

1 cup milk

2 tablespoons light corn syrup

Pinch of salt

1½ cups coarsely chopped pecans

6 tablespoons unsalted butter

2 teaspoons pure vanilla extract

Line a baking sheet with parchment or buttered waxed paper.

In a medium-size heavy saucepan, combine the two sugars, milk, corn syrup, and salt. Bring the mixture to a boil over medium-high heat, stirring constantly, then add the pecans. Hang a candy thermometer over the side of the pan and cook, uncovered, over medium-low heat, stirring frequently, until the mixture reaches 238°F to 240°F, or forms a soft ball when a small amount is dropped in ice water. Immediately remove the pan from the heat, then remove the candy thermometer and wash it in hot water.

Add the butter and vanilla and beat vigorously until the mixture loses its glossy sheen and thickens. Working quickly, drop the mixture by tablespoonfuls onto the prepared baking sheet to make rounds that spread to about 2 inches in diameter. (If the mixture begins to harden, place the pan over very low heat to soften it.) Cool the pralines completely before removing them from the paper. Store in an airtight container at room temperature. **Makes about 2 dozen pralines**.

Sazerac

It is claimed that the concept and the term "cocktail" were conceived in New Orleans during the early nineteenth century, and the Sazerac was one of the earliest creations. Originally concocted with absinthe, a wormwood-based liqueur that is now illegal, and two brands of bitters (Angostura and Peychaud), this cocktail has been revised for modern tastes. It was traditionally served straight up in an old-fashioned glass but it can also be poured over ice.

½ teaspoon anise-flavored
   liqueur (Pernod, Ricard, or
   Herbsaint)

1 teaspoon super-fine sugar

¼ teaspoon bitters

¼ cup (2 ounces) rye, bourbon,
   or blended whiskey

1 thin strip lemon zest,
   for garnish (optional)

Pour the liqueur into the bottom of a 6- to 8-ounce old-fashioned glass, swirling to coat the bottom and sides.

Fill a cocktail shaker with cracked ice, then add the sugar, bitters, and whiskey. Shake vigorously to blend, then strain the mixture into the prepared glass. Garnish with a twist of lemon zest, if desired. **Serves 1**.

Hurricane

Most visitors to New Orleans find time to stop in at
Pat O'Brien's bar for a hurricane, a fruit-based rum punch served in a tall glass
shaped like a hurricane lamp. And since New Orleans not only
doesn't prohibit drinking in the streets but actually seems to encourage it, you're
allowed to carry out a second drink in a paper cup with you to your
next destination. The original recipe is made with red passion fruit syrup, which is
difficult to find; Hawaiian Punch produces almost identical results.

¾ cup Hawaiian Punch

4 teaspoons fresh lemon juice

¼ cup (2 ounces) dark rum

*Half orange slice, for garnish
(optional)*

*Maraschino cherry, for garnish
(optional)*

In a cocktail shaker, combine the Hawaiian Punch, lemon juice, and rum. Shake vigorously to blend, then pour into a tall stemmed glass packed with cracked ice. Garnish with the orange slice and a maraschino cherry, if desired. Serve with a straw. **Serves 1**.

Café Brûlot

This is another famous creation from Jules Alciatore for
his patrons at Antoine's. It represents a fitting finale to the kind of grand-style
dining that was popular in New Orleans during the late nineteenth
century. The drink makes an impressive tableside presentation, especially if
the room is darkened as the alcohol is flamed.

8 whole cloves

*One 3½-inch piece cinnamon
stick, broken in half*

*Zest of 1 lemon, cut into long
strips ¼ inch wide*

1½ tablespoons sugar

*6 tablespoons (3 ounces) Cognac
or brandy*

3 cups strong hot coffee

In a medium-size saucepan or a chafing
dish set over an alcohol flame, combine the
cloves, cinnamon stick, lemon zest, sugar, and
Cognac. Heat over medium heat, stirring
frequently, for about 2 to 3 minutes, or until
hot. Remove the pan from the heat.

Carefully light the liquid using a long
fireplace match. Let the mixture burn for about
2 minutes. Pour the hot coffee into the
brandy mixture to extinguish the flames.

To serve, ladle the mixture into demitasse
cups. **Serves 6**.

Plantation Milk Punch

This soothing old-fashioned drink is a streamlined version of eggnog.
It is traditionally served as an eye-opener for breakfast or brunch in New Orleans
and is considered a cure for overimbibing the night before.

¾ cup half-and-half or
 light cream

2 teaspoons confectioners' sugar

¼ teaspoon pure vanilla extract

3 tablespoons (1½ ounces)
 brandy

Pinch of grated nutmeg,
 for garnish (optional)

In a blender or cocktail shaker, combine the half-and-half, sugar, vanilla, and brandy. Blend or shake vigorously to combine, then pour into a stemmed glass packed with cracked ice. Sprinkle with nutmeg, if desired. **Serves 1**.

GLOSSARY

Andouille (ahn-DOO-ee): A lean, spicy Cajun smoked pork sausage, andouille is unlike its French namesake in that it contains no chitterlings or tripe. It is traditionally used to flavor Cajun and Creole specialties such as gumbo and jambalaya.

Beignet (bin-YEAH): A small square doughnut liberally sprinkled with confectioners' sugar and served warm. (*Beignet* means "fritter" in French.)

Blackened: Chef Paul Prudhomme coined this term to describe his method of cooking fish by first rubbing it with a mixture of ground hot pepper and herbs, then searing it in a super-hot cast-iron skillet to create a charred and blackened exterior.

Calas (KAL-us): These round cakes are made with flour and rice, flavored with cinnamon, and fried. They are usually served for breakfast with syrup.

Cayenne: Also called red pepper, cayenne is a very pungent, finely ground spice made from various dried chili peppers. It is used extensively in south Louisiana cooking.

Corn flour: Used primarily in the southern United States, corn flour is finely ground cornmeal, milled from the whole kernel of corn. It can be either white or yellow and is usually used to coat foods for deep frying.

Courtbouillon (COO-be-yon): In south Louisiana, courtbouillon is a stew of fish (traditionally redfish) simmered in a roux-thickened sauce made with fish stock, tomatoes, and other vegetables such as onions and bell peppers.

Crawfish: Also known as crayfish, crawdads, and mudbugs, crawfish are freshwater crustaceans ranging in length from 3 to 6 inches and resembling tiny lobsters. Louisiana is known as the crawfish capital of the country.

Creole mustard: A golden-brown mustard made from crushed or ground mustard seed, vinegar, and salt. It has a mellow, full-bodied, moderately spicy flavor.

Creole sauce: One of the oldest and most traditional sauces in the regional lexicon, Creole sauce is made primarily with tomatoes, onions, bell peppers, and garlic; unlike most other sauces in Cajun and Creole cooking, it is not thickened with roux. It probably owes its origins more to Spanish cooking than to French.

En papillote (ahn pop-ee-YOTE): A method of cooking meat, fish, poultry, and vegetables inside a sealed parchment package. As the food cooks, the steam is trapped inside the package, enhancing the flavor of the food by sealing in its natural juices. At the table, it is split open to allow the steam to escape.

Etouffé(e) (ay-too-FAY): Literally "smothered" in French, this word describes a seafood, meat, or vegetable dish that is covered in a rich roux-thickened sauce containing garlic, onions, and bell peppers.

Filé (FEE-lay): Made from the powdered dried leaves of the sassafras tree, filé is a mild-flavored seasoning used primarily to thicken and color gumbos.

Green onion: A vegetable with a long thin green stem and a small white elongated bulb at its base; both parts are edible. Also known as a scallion or spring onion, it is always called a green onion in south Louisiana.

Grillade (gree-YOD): A lean slice of veal, beef, or pork that is pounded thin, browned, then simmered in a gravy thickened with a dark roux. In New Orleans, grillades are almost always partnered with grits and are usually served with breakfast or brunch rather than with dinner.

Grits: Coarsely ground hominy (dried hulled corn) that is slowly boiled in water or milk until soft and thick. Grits are traditionally served with breakfast and lunch.

Gumbo: A thick, strongly flavored stewlike dish made with a dark roux and any combination of shellfish, chicken, turkey, ham, duck, and sausage. It is thickened with filé powder or okra (rarely with both together) and is often served over rice.

Jambalaya (jum-buh-LIE-ya): A culinary cousin of Spanish paella, jambalaya is made with a base of rice, onions, bell peppers, and tomatoes, and flavored with various combinations of pork, ham, sausage, shrimp, crawfish, and seasonings. (The word is believed to have come from both the Spanish *jamón* and the French *jambon*, for "ham," and the African *ya*, meaning "rice.")

Maque choux (mock SHOE): A vegetable dish made with fresh corn, tomatoes, onions, bell peppers, and seasonings. Maque choux was probably passed to the Cajuns from the neighboring Choctaw Indians. (The name may be a Cajun corruption of the Choctaw term *matache*, meaning "spotted," a reference to the bits of tomato that spot the corn in cooking.)

Mirliton (MEER-luh-ton): A green, hard-skinned pear-shaped vegetable from the cucumber family. In south Louisiana, it is frequently baked and stuffed with a well-seasoned mixture of ground meat, crab, or shrimp. In Latin America and the Caribbean, mirlitons are called chayotes, vegetable pears, or christophenes.

Muffaletta: An overstuffed sandwich made with a large loaf of round Italian bread filled with Italian cold cuts, cheeses, and olive salad.

Pain perdu (pan pair-DOO): New Orleans French toast, made from thickly sliced leftover French bread soaked in an egg/milk mixture, then fried in butter. (The name means "lost bread" in French, a reference to the fact that the bread is temporarily out of sight as it soaks.)

Po'boy: New Orleans's answer to the hero or submarine sandwich, the po'boy is a long loaf of French bread or rolls filled with fried oysters, roast beef and gravy, ham, soft-shell crabs, or a combination of these ingredients. It originated in the Great Depression as a good cheap way to fill a hungry stomach.

Pralines (PRAW-leens): Unlike its brittle French cousin, the Louisiana praline is a soft, chewy candy patty made from brown sugar, butter, milk or cream, and pecans. Pralines are sold in souvenir, candy, and gift shops all over New Orleans.

Roux (roo): Roux ~ flour browned with butter or other fats such as oil or lard ~ is the essence of Cajun and Creole cooking. (The name comes from the French for "brown butter," *roux beurre*.) Its main function in Louisiana cooking is to add a deep rich flavor to a dish and to slightly thicken the cooking liquid. Color and flavor of a roux are determined by the length of cooking time ~ the longer it cooks, the deeper both will be. The ratio of flour to fat depends on the dish in which it is being used. Animal fat ~ lard or clarified butter ~ has traditionally been used, but today lighter oils are often substituted.

Instructions for cooking times vary widely. In the past, a roux was stirred constantly over very low heat for a long time, sometimes for up to an hour, and stored at a cool temperature. It was made in large batches for use over the course of several days or weeks. Most modern recipes advise cooking it for 10 minutes or less, over a higher heat, whisking almost constantly and watching very carefully

to prevent burning. As soon as the desired color is reached, the next ingredient ~ usually chopped vegetables ~ is added immediately, or the roux is removed from the heat and stirred to prevent burning. Cooking times, however, do still vary greatly, depending on the amount of roux, type of pan, temperature, humidity, and reliability of the heat source.

Sauce piquante (pea-KAHNT): A spicy roux-thickened Cajun sauce made primarily with tomatoes and a bit of vinegar, used for cooking meat, chicken, duck, and other game. It is sometimes spelled "piquant."

Tasso (TAH-so): Smoked Cajun ham that is cured with cayenne and other herbs and spices. Because of its intense spicy flavor, it is used sparingly, almost always as a seasoning element in soups, stews, or pastas. Hormel's "Cure 81" ham is a good substitute.

WEIGHTS

OUNCES AND POUNDS	METRICS
¼ ounce	7 grams
⅓ ounce	10 grams
½ ounce	14 grams
1 ounce	28 grams
1½ ounces	42 grams
1¾ ounces	50 grams
2 ounces	57 grams
3 ounces	85 grams
3½ ounces	100 grams
4 ounces (¼ pound)	114 grams
6 ounces	170 grams
8 ounces (½ pound)	227 grams
9 ounces	250 grams
16 ounces (1 pound)	464 grams

LIQUID MEASURES

tsp.: teaspoon
Tbs.: tablespoon

SPOONS AND CUPS	METRIC EQUIVALENTS
¼ tsp.	1.23 milliliters
½ tsp.	2.5 milliliters
¾ tsp.	3.7 milliliters
1 tsp.	5 milliliters
1 dessertspoon	10 milliliters
1 Tbs. (3 tsp.)	15 milliliters
2 Tbs. (1 ounce)	30 milliliters
¼ cup	60 milliliters
⅓ cup	80 milliliters
½ cup	120 milliliters
⅔ cup	160 milliliters
¾ cup	180 milliliters
1 cup (8 ounces)	240 milliliters
2 cups (1 pint)	480 milliliters
3 cups	720 milliliters
4 cups (1 quart)	1 liter
4 quarts (1 gallon)	3¾ liters

TEMPERATURES

°F (FAHRENHEIT)	°C (CENTIGRADE OR CELSIUS)
32 (water freezes)	0
200	95
212 (water boils)	100
250	120
275	135
300 (slow oven)	150
325	160
350 (moderate oven)	175
375	190
400 (hot oven)	205
425	220
450 (very hot oven)	232
475	245
500 (extremely hot oven)	260

LENGTH

U.S. MEASUREMENTS	METRIC EQUIVALENTS
⅛ inch	3 mm
¼ inch	6 mm
⅜ inch	1 cm
½ inch	1.2 cm
¾ inch	2 cm
1 inch	2.5 cm
1¼ inches	3.1 cm
1½ inches	3.7 cm
2 inches	5 cm
3 inches	7.5 cm
4 inches	10 cm
5 inches	12.5 cm

APPROXIMATE EQUIVALENTS

1 kilo is slightly more than 2 pounds
1 liter is slightly more than 1 quart
1 meter is slightly over 3 feet
1 centimeter is approximately ⅜ inch

INDEX